IN THE KITCHEN WITH

Miss Piggy

by Moi

Jim Henson Productions, Inc.
New York, New York

TIME®
LIFE
BOOKS

Time-Life Books
Alexandria, Virginia

Moi would like to thank all of the darling people who worked on this cookbook: my celebrity friends for contributing their delicious recipes, Citymeals-on-Wheels, my dear friend and visionary Jim Lewis, and the man who makes it all happen, Frank Oz.

Second printing. Printed in U.S.A.

Library of Congress Cataloging-in-Publication Data
In the kitchen with Miss Piggy : fabulous recipes from my famous celebrity
    friends / by moi.
        p. cm.
    Includes index.
    ISBN 0-7835-4781-1
    1. Cookery. 2. Celebrities. I. Time-Life Books.
TX714.15 1996
641.5--dc20   95-52383

 *o* **Kermit,**

who has always been

the hottest dish in moi's life.

Contents

Lovely Lena Horne shares a recipe for Strawberry and Champagne Sorbet on page 110!

For those with a sweet tooth, like moi, skip ahead to page 116 for Martha Stewart's Gingerbread recipe!

Turn to page 56 for Liz Taylor's fabulous Spicy Chicken!

See Sam Waterston's son's Famous Omelet recipe on page 60. It's eggs-cellent!

Sensational Side Dishes and Sauces 80

Divine Desserts 102

Etc.

Dear Friends,

Every year Citymeals-on-Wheels brings more than one million hand-delivered meals to the doors of homebound elderly people who can no longer shop or cook for themselves. Each meal is a caring message of reassurance. Throughout America, thousands of similar meals are lovingly prepared and delivered every day. Proceeds from this book will help Citymeals-on-Wheels and other private fund-raising efforts in several cities across the country.

Thank you for helping us to maintain this vital lifeline of food and human company.

Sincerely yours,

Marcia Stein
Executive Director
Citymeals-on-Wheels, New York City

Introduction

◆

**When I was approached to write this cookbook, moi thought:
Why not? If Oprah can do it...**

So here's moi's recipe for a perfect cookbook:

Ingredients:

8 Actors	11 Actresses	10 TV Personalities
3 Recording Artists	1 Poet	2 Professional Athletes
2 Supermodels	1 Flautist	2 Ice Cream Moguls
1 Retired 4-Star General	1 Former First Lady	1 Fashion Designer
1 Playwright	1 Vice Presidential Spouse	2 Opera Singers
1 Food Critic	1 Gourmet Chef	1 Writer
1 Frog	1 Cartoonist	1 Cellist
1 Martha Stewart	1 Ivana	1 Movie Director

Directions:

1. Have your people call their people and ask for a recipe for your book. Also find out if there is a part for you in their upcoming movie or television show.

2. Select your wardrobe for the all-important cover photo.

3. Take a long vacation while your assistants do all that book publishing stuff.

Bon Appétit!

Moi salutes any gadget or gismo that makes life simpler.

Miss Piggy's

Moi's Gadget Drawer

◆

❧ **HAIR DRYER:** For thawing frozen foods. Also handy for clearing crumbs from the counter.

❧ **FIRE EXTINGUISHER:** In case your roast is a teensy bit overcooked.

Note: For a tasty dessert topping, fill extinguisher with whipped cream, aim hose at your favorite dessert, spray, and enjoy!

❧ **CONCEALER:** For hiding meat loaf blemishes and other cooking imperfections.

❧ **SELF-TANNING LOTION:** For browning food.

❧ **CURLING IRON:** For turning spaghetti into rotini.

❧ **DISHWASHER:** Mine's name is Hans.

❧ **DOG:** For cleaning the kitchen floor.

❧ **SUNLAMP:** For crème brûlée.

❧ **MAGIC 8 BALL:** For choosing the right wine.

Miss Piggy's Perfect Pantry

◆

THIS LITTLE PIGGY
WENT TO MARKET...

Moi has learned to be prepared for life's little unexpected surprises. Among things that could strike without warning are hunger pangs, unannounced visitors, and other natural disasters. Stock up!

Moi's Grocery List

Chocolate
Ice Cream
Cookies and Cream
Whipped Cream
Heavy Cream
Creamsicles
Marshmallow Cream
Cream Puffs
Cheese Puffs

Chocolate
BAR GRAPH

Statistics are based on Miss Piggy's chocolate purchases in 1 calendar year.

There are three things I must have at all times: the upper hand in a relationship, an agent who returns my calls, and an ample supply of chocolate. A balanced diet always includes a variety of chocolate, and a legitimate cookbook always includes a bar graph....

Note: This graph does not include gifts from friends or fans—gifts may be sent to **Miss Piggy 117 E. 69th St. New York, NY 10021**

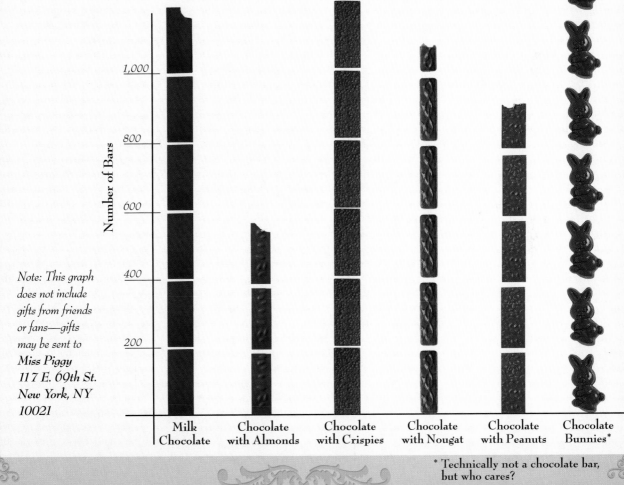

Number of Bars

1,000
800
600
400
200

Milk Chocolate · Chocolate with Almonds · Chocolate with Crispies · Chocolate with Nougat · Chocolate with Peanuts · Chocolate Bunnies*

* Technically not a chocolate bar, but who cares?

Miss Piggy's Guide to Entertaining

◆

The real secret to the table is the seating chart. Traditionally, the seating chart at a dinner party is boy-girl-boy-girl. But who cares about tradition when John Travolta and Harry Belafonte are coming to dinner? As you can see by the chart, moi has devised an ingenious boy-boy-boy-MOI-boy-boy-boy-boy seating arrangement. Squeeze in the ladies at a card table near the kitchen....

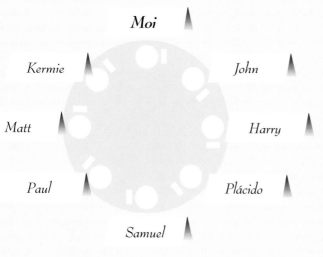

Moi

Kermie   John

Matt   Harry

Paul   Plácido

Samuel

❧ THE TABLECLOTH: A white tablecloth by itself is a dining table in its underwear. To properly dress the table, simply cover it with food until there are no white spaces showing.

Moi prefers satin tablecloths. The slippery sheen of the cloth makes sliding the serving dishes around the table much easier. With a long table, you can get a really good run on a casserole.

❧ PLACEMATS: Mirrored placemats nicely complement the table, and how comforting it is to see someone as familiar as oneself at a dinner party!

The hostess should always be the center of attention at the table—moi recommends a spotlight to achieve this effect.

❧ THE CENTERPIECE: *Avoidance:* A centerpiece is perfect for avoiding eye contact with certain guests.

For privacy: Duck behind the centerpiece to remove food from your teeth.

❧ FINGER BOWLS: Finger bowls are for finger foods: M&Ms, chocolate-covered almonds, little mints, chocolate kisses.

❧ MOOD LIGHTING: With Kermit, moi prefers candlelight or moonlight. Without Kermit, a bare light bulb will do just fine.

❧ TRIVETS: I have no idea what the heck they are.

❧ MUSIC: Depending on your budget there are several ways to go:

High Budget:	Full Orchestra
Fairly High Budget:	String Quartet
Moderate Budget:	Pianist
Low Budget:	Accordion
Really Low Budget:	Humming

❧ NAPKIN RINGS: If you can't wear it on your wrist or your finger, why bother?

Miss Piggy's Guide to Food and Fashion

◆

**Food and fashion go together like milk and cookies...
Fred and Ginger...Roy and Trigger....**

SELECTING A HANDBAG:

If you plan to take a snack for the long ride home, make sure the purse is up to the task. Moi suggests one of those trendy little backpacks in which form follows function.

LEFTOVERS:

Why put off till tomorrow what you can eat today? Put your aluminum foil to better use, like this fabulous dress by my close personal friend and designer, Reynoldo Rapp.

Moi always tries to coordinate my outfit with my food.

Scrumptious Soups and Salads

◆

Little Hellos to Your Stomach

For a Tuna Health Salad
fit for a King, turn to page 26.

Whoopi Goldberg's Peas Porridge Hot, Peas Porridge Cold

"A loaf of crusty French bread and voilà! You've got a meal for royalty."

–W. G.

4 tablespoons butter

½ cup cooking oil (preferably French nut oil)

2 onions, chopped

2 garlic cloves, chopped

5 medium-size potatoes, peeled and sliced

2 to 3 quarts chicken stock (preferably homemade)

7 carrots, peeled and quartered

2 stalks celery, cut in half

¼ pound French string beans (haricots verts) or green beans

3 leeks, cleaned and cut into pieces

2 large zucchini or 3 small green squash, cut into chunks

¼ head cauliflower, broken apart

2 bay leaves

pinch to ¼ teaspoon ground nutmeg

salt and pepper

heavy cream

parsley sprigs

Whoopi Goldberg

I have been a friend and fan of Whoopi's for years. How many wonderful awards she has amassed in that time. But truly the greatest honor of all is to have a line of cushions named after you....

1. Melt the butter in a large pot. Stir in the oil. Add the onions and garlic; cook until golden. Add the potatoes and cook until browned. Add the chicken stock, remaining vegetables, bay leaves, and nutmeg, salt, and pepper to taste. Bring to a boil; reduce the heat to very low and simmer 2 hours or until the vegetables are good and soft.

2. Remove the vegetables from the pot with a ladle, discarding the bay leaves. Put the vegetables through a food mill or purée, in batches, in a food processor or blender at low speed. Return them to the pot. Adjust the salt and pepper and reheat. Dish out into bowls, topping each serving with a generous tablespoonful of heavy cream.

This may be served hot in the winter, ice cold in the summer. A small sprig of parsley compliments the celadon green color beautifully.

Over the years, you will adjust this recipe to your own taste. I like to add half a package of frozen peas to ensure the pale green color.

Serves 12

Katie Couric

I *have always enjoyed being interviewed by my dear, close friend Katie. Then one day I asked her: "What is your secret to being so chipper and so perky so early in the morning?" All I got was this recipe for soup....*

Katie Couric's Zesty Tomato-Thyme Soup

1 medium-size onion

2 garlic cloves

2 stalks celery

¼ cup packed parsley sprigs (optional)

1 tablespoon olive oil or vegetable oil

2 16-ounce cans crushed tomatoes

1½ cups chicken broth

2 tablespoons tomato paste

2 teaspoons grated orange zest

1 teaspoon dried thyme

¼ teaspoon pepper

¼ to ½ cup sour cream, to taste

1. Coarsely chop the onion and garlic in a food processor. Remove the mixture; set aside. Then chop the celery and parsley (if using) in the processor. Remove and set aside.

2. In a large saucepan, warm the oil on medium-high heat until hot but not smoking. Add the onion and garlic and stir-fry until the mixture begins to brown, about 5 minutes. Stir in the tomatoes and their juice, the chicken broth, tomato paste, orange zest, thyme, pepper, and the chopped celery and parsley (if using). Bring to a boil; then reduce the heat to medium-low, cover, and simmer for at least 10 minutes. Serve hot, at room temperature, or slightly chilled, but not cold. Offer with a dollop of sour cream on top.

To save time (which I'm always looking to do), you could make this in the microwave. Here's how: Combine the oil, chopped onion, garlic, celery, and parsley (if using) in a 3-quart microwave-safe casserole. Cover loosely and cook at 100% for 4 minutes. Stir in the tomatoes and their juice, the chicken broth, tomato paste, orange zest, thyme, and pepper. Cover and cook at 100% for 6 minutes or until it comes to a boil. Cook at 50% for 7 minutes to blend the flavors.

Serves 6

Cheryl Tiegs's Borscht

2 medium-size red onions, chopped

1 tablespoon canola oil

1 pound beef stew meat, trimmed
   of fat and cubed

4 cups water

4 cups strong beef broth or consommé

1 teaspoon dried thyme

1 bay leaf

2 medium-size beets, peeled and diced

2 carrots, peeled and diced

1 tablespoon red wine vinegar

½ teaspoon salt

½ to 1 teaspoon pepper

3 parsley sprigs, chopped

4 ounces sour cream

1. In a large saucepan, sauté the onions in oil over medium-high heat until golden brown. Add the beef, water, broth, thyme, and bay leaf. Simmer gently for 1½ hours or until the beef is very tender, adding water if necessary. Add the beets and simmer for 10 more minutes. Add the carrots and vinegar; simmer for 15 more minutes.

2. Remove the bay leaf, sprinkle with salt and pepper to taste, and stir in the parsley.

Serve the soup hot in bowls with sour cream on the side.

Serves 4

A Tip from Moi:
A lot of you have written to moi asking how to get borscht out of your carpet. It's quite simple. You can't.

Cheryl Tiegs

As close friends and cover girls, Cheryl and I have always swapped makeup tips, fashion tips, cooking tips, and Q-tips, and now we'd like to share a revolutionary new beauty tip: A heaping bowl of Cheryl's borscht gives you pep, energy, and radiant red lip color that lasts all day long.

Miss Piggy

Brooke Shields

*M*y dearest friend Brookie and I have worked together in the movies and on TV, so naturally moi was excited to see her Broadway debut in Grease. Brookie asked my honest opinion, and I'll be perfectly frank, the snack selection in the theater lobby was lousy. But her performance was très magnifique!

Brooke Shields's Vegetable Health Soup

2 large sprinkles Mrs. Dash

1 large onion, chopped

2 medium-size Granny Smith apples, peeled, cored, and chopped

vegetable oil spray

Any 1 of the following 3 vegetables:

   1 large bunch broccoli (do not throw stems away)

   1 large head of cauliflower

   1 large bunch carrots

1 46-ounce can chicken broth (skim fat from top)

low-fat cottage cheese (optional)

parsley or mint sprigs

1. Sprinkle Mrs. Dash on onion and apples. In a nonstick frying pan lightly sprayed with vegetable oil, sauté onion and apples until softened. Set aside.

2. Clean vegetable and chop into 1-inch pieces. Steam or parboil vegetable. Pour broth into a large saucepan. Add all ingredients except cheese and parsley. Simmer for 10 minutes. Purée mixture in batches in a blender.

May be served hot or cold with a dab of cottage cheese (if using) in the center. Garnish with parsley in the winter, mint in the summer.

Serves 5

A Tip from Moi:

If vous are going to add Mrs. Dash, please make sure Mr. Dash doesn't mind....

Larry King's Favorite Tuna Health Salad

2 6½-ounce cans water-packed tuna

2 tablespoons each diced sweet onion, green bell pepper, celery, and tomato

1 tablespoon whipped nonfat salad dressing

1 tablespoon corn oil

¼ cup white wine vinegar

Rinse and drain tuna. Combine all ingredients in a bowl and toss gently.

For a serving option, display the tuna on a bed of lettuce garnished with sliced Bermuda onion and tomatoes.

Serves 4

"It's the world's best lunch. I eat this at least three times a week."

–L. K.

Larry King

Moi loves sweet, darling Lawrence for his devastating wit, his sparkling personality, and his suave demeanor. The very thought makes me want to rush right out and buy Kermit a pair of suspenders—of course, first I'd have to rush right out and buy him a pair of pants.

My darling, athletic Andre. How I love the strawberries and cream at Wimbledon…the quiche Lorraine at the French Open…the cheese fries at Flushing Meadow. How I love the way you frequently use the word love when vous are working….

Andre Agassi

Andre Agassi's Tomato and Mozzarella Salad

2 pounds very ripe tomatoes, cored and sliced

4 ounces fresh mozzarella, thinly sliced

8 to 12 fresh basil leaves

2 tablespoons extra-virgin olive oil

salt and freshly ground black pepper

Arrange tomatoes and mozzarella, alternating slices, on 4 salad plates. Tuck basil leaves among the slices. Drizzle each salad with some of the oil and sprinkle lightly with salt and pepper.

Serves 4

Harvey Fierstein

*M*y precious Harveletto is a wonderful cook, a great actor, and a Tony award-winning play-wright. I often dream of bringing home a Tony, but for now moi will settle for a Kermie....

Harvey Fierstein's Tomato and Onion Salad

4 large beefy tomatoes, thickly sliced

1 red onion, thinly sliced

1 egg yolk

1 tablespoon balsamic vinegar

1 garlic clove, crushed

½ cup extra-virgin olive oil

2 tablespoons tepid water

2 tablespoons Dijon mustard

1 large bunch fresh basil, chopped

Arrange the tomatoes and onion on a serving platter. Stir together the remaining ingredients until well combined. Spread over the tomatoes and onion and let sit at room temperature for at least an hour. YUMMY!

Serves 6 to 8

If you are concerned about the possible health risks of raw eggs, substitute 1 tablespoon mayonnaise for the egg yolk.

Lauren Bacall's Spinach and Sesame Salad

½ cup chicken broth

1 tablespoon sesame seeds

1 tablespoon tahini (sesame paste)

1 teaspoon dark sesame oil

1½ tablespoons low-sodium soy sauce

1 tablespoon fresh lemon juice

1 teaspoon peeled and finely chopped fresh ginger

1 pound spinach, washed, stemmed, and dried

¼ pound mushrooms, wiped clean and thinly sliced (about 1 cup)

1 large ripe tomato, sliced into thin wedges

salt

freshly ground black pepper

1. Boil the chicken broth in a small saucepan until only 2 tablespoons remain, about 7 minutes. At the same time, toast the sesame seeds in a small ungreased skillet over medium-low heat until golden, about 3 minutes. Set the sesame seeds aside.

2. Make the dressing by mixing the tahini and sesame oil in a small bowl. Whisk in the reduced chicken broth, soy sauce, lemon juice, and ginger.

3. Put the spinach and mushrooms in a large bowl. Sprinkle the tomatoes with salt and pepper and add to the bowl. Pour the dressing over all of it, grind in some more pepper, and toss well. Scatter the sesame seeds over the salad and serve.

Serves 6

My glamorous and dear, dear friend "Betty" and moi are renaissance women, gracing both stage and screen. Her Spinach and Sesame Salad is perfect for her svelte figure. Of course, for more full-figured women, like moi, some fries and a burrito make it all happen.

Matt Lauer

Matthew is such a wonderful journalist. He's intelligent, charming, eloquent, and entertaining. Unfortunately, he's also taken....

Matt Lauer's Boston Lettuce Salad

12 thin French bread slices,
  cut into cubes

3 tablespoons extra-virgin olive oil

1 whole garlic bulb, the cloves
  separated and peeled

1 tablespoon balsamic vinegar
  (or 1 tablespoon red wine vinegar
  mixed with ¼ teaspoon honey)

1 tablespoon safflower oil

⅛ teaspoon salt

freshly ground black pepper

2 heads Boston lettuce or
  4 heads Bibb lettuce, washed
  and dried

1. Preheat oven to 400°F.

2. Toss the bread cubes in 2 tablespoons of the olive oil. Spread them out on a baking sheet and toast until golden, about 5 minutes. Set them aside.

3. Put the garlic cloves into a small saucepan and add enough water to cover them. Bring the liquid to a boil; then reduce the heat and simmer until the garlic is quite tender (about 15 minutes). Increase the heat and boil until only about 2 tablespoons of the liquid remain, 2 to 3 minutes.

4. Pour the contents of the pan into a sieve set over a small bowl. With a wooden spoon, mash the garlic through the sieve into the bowl. Whisk the vinegar into the garlic mixture; then add the remaining 1 tablespoon olive oil, the safflower oil, salt, and pepper to taste.

5. Combine the lettuce and the toasted bread cubes. Toss them with the dressing. Serve at once.

Serves 6

Marvelous Main Courses

◆

The Big Kahuna

With style and flair, Ivana and Miss Piggy
whip up a fabulous Beef Goulash on page 66.

Candice Bergen's Tortellini Salad

1 small yellow or red bell pepper,
   halved and seeded

1 small green bell pepper, halved and seeded

1 small zucchini, halved lengthwise

½ small red onion, cut into thick rings

2 tablespoons lemon juice

1 teaspoon grated lemon zest (optional)

¼ cup olive oil or vegetable oil

1 tablespoon Dijon mustard

½ teaspoon dillweed

⅛ teaspoon salt

⅛ teaspoon pepper

pinch of sugar

1½ cups dried cheese-filled tortellini
   (about 6 ounces)

5 cherry tomatoes, halved

3 scallions, finely chopped

1. Grill or broil the bell peppers, zucchini, and onion until well browned and tender. Chop them into bite-size pieces. Set aside.

2. Bring a large pot of water to a boil.

3. Meanwhile, place the lemon juice and zest (if using) in a large salad bowl. Whisk in the oil, mustard, dillweed, salt, pepper, and sugar to make the vinaigrette.

4. Add the pasta to the boiling water and cook until al dente, 10 to 12 minutes, or according to the package directions.

5. Drain the pasta and add it to the vinaigrette. Add the grilled vegetables, tomatoes, and scallions. Toss well to combine. Serve the salad warm or at room temperature.

Serves 4

Candice Bergen

Lovely Candice gets an Emmy for everything. She will probably even get an Emmy for best recipe in a celebrity cookbook written by a superstar pig!

Clint Eastwood

Dearest Clinty is adorable, intelligent, and tall. I have such great respect for actors who become Academy Award-winning directors, and even greater respect for Academy Award-winning directors who give moi really big parts in their movies!

Clint Eastwood's Spaghetti Western

juice of ½ lemon

12 tablespoons olive oil

12 baby artichokes

½ pound spaghetti

2 large garlic cloves, diced

¼ cup finely chopped celery

¼ cup chopped shallots

½ cup tomato purée

½ cup fish stock

salt and freshly ground black pepper

¼ teaspoon dried thyme

1 bay leaf

2 tablespoons fresh parsley, chopped

saffron

2 tablespoons tomato paste

½ teaspoon anchovy paste

4 clams, chopped

4 Monterey Bay prawns or jumbo shrimp

12 large mussels

½ cup brandy

1 yellow pepper, thinly sliced

1 red pepper, thinly sliced

2½ tablespoons Pernod

½ cup heavy cream

8 large, very fresh sea scallops, quartered

If you are concerned about the possible health risks of raw seafood, omit the scallops.

1. Stir juice from ½ lemon and 2 tablespoons of the olive oil into a large pot of boiling salted water. Add artichokes and boil for 5 minutes or until almost tender. Remove artichokes with a slotted spoon and rinse under cold running water. Reserve artichoke cooking water. Peel outer leaves from 8 artichokes down to the most tender part (leave 4 artichokes with leaves intact). Cut off stems. Cut peeled artichokes into bite-size pieces (about 1½ inches long). Set aside.

2. Add additional salted water to leftover artichoke water, bring to a boil, and cook spaghetti until al dente. Drain and return to pot. Set aside.

3. In a large sauté pan, heat 7 tablespoons olive oil; sauté garlic, celery, and 2 tablespoons shallots until golden. Add tomato purée, fish stock, salt and pepper, thyme, bay leaf, parsley, 2 generous pinches saffron, tomato paste, anchovy paste, and clams. Bring to a low simmer and cover.

4. In another large sauté pan, heat 3 tablespoons olive oil and sauté 2 tablespoons chopped shallots. Season with black pepper. Add prawns and mussels, cover with brandy, and ignite. Remove from heat and when flame subsides, set aside.

5. Add red and yellow peppers, artichoke pieces, and mussels with their cooking liquid to the sauce and simmer 5 minutes. Add Pernod and cream to sauce and cook 1 minute, stirring constantly. Remove from heat.

6. Using a slotted spoon, remove peppers from sauce and add to spaghetti. Rinse the spaghetti-pepper mixture in hot water and drain (this is to remove traces of the sauce).

7. Cover the bottom of 4 flat bowls with a few tablespoons of sauce. Arrange a quarter of the spaghetti in each bowl, leaving a hollow in the center. Place 2 quartered raw scallops in the center. With a slotted spoon, remove the mussels from the sauce and arrange 3 mussels on the edge of each serving. On the opposite side, place 3 artichoke slices, similarly extracted from the sauce. Place a reserved, uncut artichoke over the scallops. Remove bay leaf from sauce and discard. Spoon sauce over scallops and mussels. Place 1 prawn in center. If preparing in advance, cover with foil and set aside. To serve, reheat in 325°F oven for 20 minutes.

Serves 4

Lauren Hutton

My dear, close friend and fellow cover girl Lauren and I used to have a little feud going on: Whoever graced the most magazine covers each month bought the other one dinner. But we had to stop, because Lauren said it was getting too expensive.

Lauren Hutton's Linguine with Pesto

2 garlic cloves

¼ cup pine nuts

about ½ teaspoon salt

2 cups packed basil leaves

⅓ cup extra-virgin olive oil

½ cup grated Parmesan cheese

1 pound red potatoes, peeled

1 pound linguine

½ pound snow peas

1. In a food processor, combine garlic, pine nuts, and ½ teaspoon of the salt. Process to a paste.

2. Add basil and drizzle oil in a steady stream through tube of food processor, continuing to blend until pesto is very smooth and no large pieces of basil are visible.

3. Transfer basil mixture to a bowl and stir in Parmesan by hand. Set aside.

4. Boil potatoes until tender. Drain. Cut into bite-size pieces.

5. Cook pasta according to package directions. About 1 minute before pasta is done, add snow peas to water. Continue to cook until pasta is al dente.

6. Drain pasta and peas, reserving 2 tablespoons of the pasta water. Stir water into pesto.

7. In a large serving bowl, toss pasta, peas, potatoes, and pesto. Season to taste with salt. Serve immediately.

Serves 4

Robin Leach

Dear Robin is a great friend of all superstars. Whereas other journalists skim the surface of a story, Robin takes us for the in-depth tour of the more important things. . . like the closets. . . the bedrooms. . . the bathrooms. . . the medicine cabinets. . . .

Robin Leach's Chicken and Vegetable Pasta Salad

Chicken

1 pound boneless, skinless chicken breasts

2 tablespoons lemon juice

1 teaspoon peeled and grated fresh ginger

2 tablespoons soy sauce

2 tablespoons white wine

½ teaspoon ground ginger

½ teaspoon dried basil

2 teaspoons Butter Buds

½ teaspoon dry mustard

¼ teaspoon pepper

Stir together all the ingredients except chicken in an 8- by 8-inch glass baking dish. Add chicken and turn it over several times. Broil until firm, about 10 minutes, turning once during cooking. Let cool. Cover and refrigerate at least 1 hour. Cut chicken into 1-inch cubes.

Vegetables

¼ cup stir-fry or teriyaki sauce

2 teaspoons peeled and grated fresh ginger

1 tablespoon soy sauce

2 tablespoons white wine

1 large onion, chopped

2 bell peppers, seeded and chopped
   (use 2 different colors)

1 pound mushrooms, chopped

2 medium-size zucchini, chopped

4 ounces bean sprouts

¼ cup fresh basil, chopped

In a large wok, stir together the stir-fry sauce, ginger, soy sauce, and white wine. Add the vegetables and basil and stir-fry over high heat until tender, about 8 minutes. Add the chicken and stir until hot. Transfer to a large serving bowl.

Pasta

½ pound angel hair pasta

1 14-ounce jar tomato-basil pasta sauce
   or 1 cup pesto

grated Parmesan cheese

pepper

8 cherry tomatoes, halved

Cook pasta in a large pan of boiling water until pasta is al dente. Toss with the vegetables and chicken. Top with sauce or pesto and Parmesan. (If it is a cold, wintry day, you may wish to warm the pasta sauce before tossing it with the other ingredients.) Season with pepper. Garnish with cherry tomatoes.

Serves 4

Diane Sawyer's Favorite Penne with Corn and Tomato Sauce

1½ tablespoons red wine vinegar

3 tablespoons olive oil, or to taste

½ cup corn kernels (cut from about
   1 ear cooked corn)

1 pound tomatoes, seeded and chopped

¼ cup thinly sliced scallions

½ pound penne or other small
   tubular pasta

salt and pepper to taste

In a large bowl, whisk together the vinegar and oil. Stir in the corn, tomatoes, and scallions. In a pan of boiling salted water, cook the penne for 8 to 10 minutes or until it is al dente. Drain it well. Add the penne to the tomato mixture and toss well. Season with salt and pepper.

Serves 2

Diane Sawyer

Diane is a master journalist, a consummate professional, and a gorgeous lady. I can't count the number of times I have been mistaken for her!

Samuel L. Jackson

Samuel is in all of those darling little shoot-'em-up movies with big sweaty men and guns. Like his movies, I'd rate his recipe "R" as in: **R you busy tonight, Samuel?**

Samuel L. Jackson's Spinach Linguine and Ground Turkey Sauce

4 tablespoons butter

8 ounces mushrooms, sliced

1 medium-size green bell pepper, diced

1 medium-size red bell pepper, diced

1 medium-size onion, diced

1 pound ground turkey

½ teaspoon garlic powder

½ teaspoon seasoning salt

1 26-ounce jar spaghetti sauce

1 pound spinach linguine

1. Melt the butter in a large skillet. Add the mushrooms, peppers, and onion. Cover and cook on low heat for 15 minutes. Set aside in a bowl.

2. Brown the turkey in the skillet, sprinkling the turkey with the garlic powder and seasoning salt. Add the vegetables and spaghetti sauce. Cover and cook on low heat for 30 minutes, stirring frequently.

3. Cook the linguine according to the package directions. Drain and mix with the sauce. Cover and cook on low heat for 3 minutes.

Serves 4 generously

Paul Newman's Tasty Thai Shrimp and Sesame Noodles

1 pound medium-size shrimp, shelled and deveined

1 8-ounce bottle Newman's Own Light Italian Dressing

2 tablespoons chunky peanut butter

1 tablespoon soy sauce

1 tablespoon honey

1 teaspoon peeled and grated fresh ginger

½ teaspoon crushed red pepper flakes

1 8-ounce package capellini or angel hair pasta

2 tablespoons salad oil

1 tablespoon sesame oil

1 medium-size carrot, peeled and shredded

1 cup chopped green onions

¼ cup chopped cilantro

Paul Newman

*P*aul is a very close
personal friend of moi's.
Most people love Paul for
his steely blue eyes, win-
ning smile, fast driving,
and incredible acting
ability. Moi loves him
for his popcorn.

1. In a medium-size bowl, mix the shrimp with ⅓ cup of the dressing. Cover and refrigerate 1 hour. In a small bowl, mix with a wire whisk or fork the peanut butter, soy sauce, honey, ginger, crushed red pepper flakes, and remaining dressing; set aside.

2. Prepare the capellini according to package directions; drain. Meanwhile, heat the salad oil and sesame oil in a 4-quart saucepan over high heat until very hot. Add the carrot and cook 1 minute. Drain off the dressing from the shrimp; discard the dressing. Add the shrimp and green onions to the carrot and cook, stirring constantly, approximately 3 minutes or until the shrimp turn opaque throughout.

3. In a large bowl, toss the hot capellini with the dressing and shrimp mixtures. Sprinkle with the cilantro. Serve immediately.

Serves 4

Note: This recipe can also be made with chicken breasts instead of shrimp. Substitute 4 medium-size boneless, skinless chicken breast halves (about 1 pound total), cut crosswise into thin strips.

Jodie Foster's Penne with Broccoli Rabe

Jodie Foster

*L*ovely Jodie is a wonderful friend. She is also a two-time Academy Award-winning actress, a distinguished direc-tor, and a beautiful woman. She has shared the screen with Sir Anthony Hopkins, Mel Gibson, James Garner, and Robert De Niro. Makes you kind of sick—don't it?!

1 pound penne

1 pound broccoli rabe, halved crosswise

2 to 3 tablespoons olive oil

2 garlic cloves, minced

½ cup grated Parmesan cheese

pinch of crushed red pepper flakes

1. In a large pot of boiling water, cook the pasta until al dente according to package directions. About 5 minutes before the pasta is done, add the broccoli rabe to the boiling water and cook until crisp-tender.

2. Meanwhile, heat the oil in a small saucepan over medium heat. Add the garlic and cook, stirring frequently, until it is lightly browned, about 2 minutes. Remove from heat.

3. Drain the pasta and broccoli rabe and put in a large serving bowl. Add the garlic mixture, Parmesan, and red pepper flakes. Toss to combine.

Serves 4

My dear friend Donna Karan is moi's favorite designer. I just adore her simple, clean, classic fashions. But a pink boa and a metallic bustier would put them over the top!

Donna Karan

Donna Karan's Garlic-Thyme Grilled Chicken

2 whole kosher or free-range chickens, cut into 8 pieces

15 garlic cloves, chopped

juice of 2 freshly squeezed lemons

⅓ cup olive oil

1 teaspoon salt

1 teaspoon freshly ground black pepper

generous pinch of red pepper flakes

1 teaspoon dried thyme

¼ cup Dijon mustard

¼ cup white wine

1. In a large bowl, combine all ingredients except chicken. Add chicken pieces, turning to coat well. Cover and refrigerate for 1 hour.

2. Remove chicken from marinade, discarding marinade, and arrange in a large baking pan. Broil, bone side up, until golden. Turn pieces and repeat. Remove chicken from broiler, lower oven temperature to 350°F, and continue to cook for 12 more minutes or until juices run clear.

Serves 8

Glenn Close

*G*lenn and I are very close friends when we are not vying for the same roles. I remember when we were up for the lead role in Sarah, Plain and Tall. Unfortunately, I had to turn it down. I would have taken the part if the movie were called Sarah, Drop-Dead Gorgeous.

Glenn Close's Chicken, Mushroom, and Barley Stew

2 tablespoons butter

3 tablespoons all-purpose flour

3 cups chicken broth

¾ teaspoon dried thyme

¼ teaspoon pepper

½ cup quick-cooking barley

2 large carrots, cut into thin slices

¼ pound mushrooms, cut into
thin slices

1 pound skinless, boneless
chicken breasts, cut into
bite-size pieces

10 cherry tomatoes

1 small bunch scallions (about 6),
coarsely chopped

1. In a large saucepan, melt the butter over medium heat. Stir in the flour. Continue cooking and stirring until the flour has completely absorbed the butter.

2. Increase the heat to medium-high, slowly add a small amount of the chicken broth, and stir to combine with the butter and flour. When there are no lumps of flour left, it is safe to add the remaining chicken broth. Also add the thyme and pepper. Bring to a boil and cook, stirring, until slightly thickened.

3. Reduce the heat to maintain a simmer, stir in the barley, and cook for 3 minutes. Add the carrots and cook for about 3 more minutes.

4. Add the mushrooms, chicken, and whole tomatoes. Return the stew to a boil over medium-high heat, breaking up the tomatoes with a spoon. Reduce the heat to medium-low, cover, and simmer until the chicken is cooked through, about 5 minutes.

5. Stir in the scallions and serve hot.

Serves 4

Tipper Gore

Darling Tipper is charismatic, energetic, smart, and stylish—so very much like moi! Now all I need is a few of those adorable Secret Service men flocking around to carry my shopping bags. . . .

Tipper Gore's Spiced Roast Chicken

mushroom stuffing (recipe below)

1 3½-pound chicken

1 tablespoon margarine or butter

⅔ cup Marsala

salt and pepper to taste

Mushroom Stuffing

2 tablespoons olive oil

1 onion, finely chopped

1 teaspoon garam masala

4 ounces chopped button mushrooms

1 cup coarsely grated parsnips

1 cup coarsely grated carrots

¼ cup minced walnuts

2 teaspoons chopped fresh thyme

1 cup fresh white bread crumbs

1 egg, beaten

salt and pepper to taste

1. Preheat oven to 375°F.

2. Prepare mushroom stuffing: In a large saucepan, heat olive oil; add onion and sauté 2 minutes or until softened. Stir in garam masala and cook 1 minute. Add mushrooms, parsnips, and carrots; cook, stirring, 5 minutes. Remove from heat; let cool 5 minutes; stir in remaining stuffing ingredients.

3. Stuff and truss chicken. Place, breast down, in a nonstick roasting pan; add ¼ cup water. Roast 45 minutes; turn chicken breast up and dot with margarine or butter. Roast about 45 minutes or until a meat thermometer inserted in thickest part of thigh (not touching bone) registers 180°F. Transfer to a platter; cover with aluminum foil to keep warm.

4. Pour off and discard fat from roasting pan; add Marsala to remaining cooking juices, scraping up any browned bits. Boil over high heat 1 minute to reduce slightly; season with salt and pepper. Pour into a pitcher.

5. Remove stuffing and place in a serving bowl. If you are watching your fat intake, remove skin from chicken. Carve chicken and serve with stuffing and flavored meat juices.

Serves 4

Elizabeth Taylor's Spicy Chicken

2 teaspoons curry powder

1 teaspoon ground cumin

½ teaspoon ground ginger

½ teaspoon turmeric

½ garlic clove, crushed

1 onion, chopped

1 teaspoon peeled and grated fresh ginger

1 3½-pound chicken, cut into 8 serving pieces and skinned

Combine dry ingredients with garlic, onion, and fresh grated ginger. Coat chicken with mixture, cover, and refrigerate for 3 hours, preferably longer. Place on moderately hot barbecue grill for 35 to 45 minutes or broil in oven approximately 25 minutes or until done, turning once.

Serves 4

A Tip from Moi:

Moi has discovered that Liz's spicy mixture also makes a tingly and tasty facial mask. Simply smooth on, wait 10 minutes, rinse, and follow with a chocolate mudpack. Voilà! Vous are ready for a night of dinner and dancing!

Elizabeth Taylor

*M*oi *is a great admirer of dearest Liz. She has
everything: timeless beauty, exquisite acting ability,
and an Academy Award. We're so much alike—well,
two out of three ain't bad.*

Pierre Franey's
Cuisses de Grenouilles Poulette
(Frogs' Legs in Cream Sauce)

8 pairs frogs' legs (about 2 pounds total)

4 tablespoons butter

2 tablespoons finely chopped shallots

½ pound mushrooms, cut into quarters
(about 3 cups)

salt and freshly ground pepper

½ cup dry white wine

1 cup heavy cream

2 teaspoons all-purpose flour

1 egg yolk, lightly beaten

juice of ½ lemon

⅛ teaspoon cayenne pepper

2 tablespoons finely chopped chives

A Word from Moi:

Darling Pierre is a fabulous friend and chef, but as you can see, moi is a teensy bit angry with him at the moment….

Pierre Franey

*F*rog's legs? Frog's legs?!
I will not comment on this
except to say, chef's legs?
How about broken legs?!

1. Pat the frogs' legs dry. Cut off and discard the bottom end of each leg.

2. Melt 2 tablespoons of the butter in a skillet large enough to hold the frogs' legs in one layer. Add the shallots and cook briefly.

3. Add the frogs' legs, mushrooms, and salt and pepper to taste. Cook, stirring, about 1 minute. Add the wine and cook 5 minutes. Transfer the frogs' legs to a warm serving platter.

4. Bring the cooking liquid to a boil over high heat and cook down to ⅓ cup. Add the cream and cook about 1 minute.

5. Blend the flour with the remaining 2 tablespoons butter. When thoroughly mixed, add this gradually to the simmering sauce. Remove the sauce from the heat and immediately beat in the egg yolk, stirring rapidly. Add the lemon juice and cayenne pepper.

6. Pour the sauce over the frogs' legs. Sprinkle with chopped chives.

Serves 4

If your dinner guest is Miss Piggy or Kermit, you'd better substitute chicken in this recipe. Use about 1½ pounds skinless, boneless chicken breasts, thinly pounded, in place of the frogs' legs.

Sam Waterston

*S*weet and talented Samuel has always been the epitome of class and style. He's a true gentleman. When we go out for dinner, he always lets moi order the large onion rings.

Graham's Famous Omelet

(as told to Sam Waterston by his son Graham)

To make this omelet you have to get three eggs, a slice of a red and a green bell pepper, three mushrooms, and three small handfuls of grated cheese.

1. Crack the eggs into a bowl; beat until fluffy. Add salt, pepper, and hot sauce to taste. Dice the bell pepper slices and the mushrooms. (Optional: Add chopped basil and/or chives and/or green onions; and 2 handfuls of chopped tomatoes, without seeds or juice.)

2. Meanwhile, heat an 8-inch omelet pan over medium-high heat. Have a large slice of butter in the pan to keep the omelet from sticking. To see when the pan is hot enough, pour in a bit of the egg. When it dries, pour in the rest. Toppings go in 30 seconds later. Dig around the sides and shake the pan to keep the omelet loose. Fold in one side and then the other. Flip to the other side; then take it out and feast.

Serves 1

Tim Curry

*S*uave Tim is a debonair actor and a charismatic performer. When he looks into my eyes and says something in that marvelous English accent, I…I can't understand a word he is saying!

Tim Curry's Lemon-Stuffed Roasted Chicken

4 tablespoons butter, melted

4 shallots, minced

3 garlic cloves, minced or crushed through a press

3 teaspoons dried thyme or dried tarragon

½ teaspoon pepper

3 lemons

1 3-pound chicken, rinsed inside and out and patted dry

½ teaspoon salt

1. Preheat the oven to 425°F. Line a roasting pan with foil.

2. In a small saucepan, combine the butter, shallots, garlic, 2 teaspoons of the herb, and ¼ teaspoon of the pepper.

3. Prick 2 of the lemons all over with a fork and then halve them. Cut the third lemon into thin slices.

4. Place the chicken on a rack in the roasting pan.

5. Sprinkle the remaining 1 teaspoon herb, the remaining ¼ teaspoon pepper, and the salt into the cavity of the chicken; then stuff the lemon halves into the cavity.

6. Arrange the lemon slices over the chicken and spoon on some of the butter mixture. Roast the chicken for 15 minutes.

7. Lower the oven temperature to 350°F and roast the chicken for another 45 minutes, basting every 15 minutes with the butter mixture and pan juices. The chicken is done when the juices run clear and the internal temperature registers 180°F on a meat thermometer inserted in the thickest part of a thigh (not touching bone).

8. Let the chicken rest for 5 to 10 minutes before carving. Serve the chicken with some of the pan juices spooned on top.

Serves 4

Kristi Yamaguchi's Chicken Scaloppine

Kristi Yamaguchi

Graceful, lithe, and charming Kristi. I was going to score this recipe just like a real figure skating judge, with compulsory and artistic merit and how pretty the dress was. But it was too complicated. So I will give it a yummy.

3 tablespoons all-purpose flour

¼ teaspoon pepper

4 chicken cutlets, pounded ¼ inch thick

1 tablespoon olive oil or vegetable oil

1 cup water

2 cups chicken broth

1 cup rice

1 tablespoon reduced-sodium soy sauce

5 quarter-size slices (¼ inch thick) fresh ginger, finely chopped

⅓ cup cilantro sprigs, finely chopped (optional)

2 garlic cloves, minced or crushed through a press

1 tablespoon honey

1 tablespoon sesame seeds

1. In a shallow bowl, combine the flour and pepper. Lightly dredge the chicken in the mixture; set aside any remaining flour.

2. In a large nonstick skillet, heat the oil over medium-high heat until oil is hot but not smoking. Add the chicken and cook, turning once, until golden brown, about 3 minutes per side. Remove the chicken to a plate and cover loosely with foil to keep warm.

3. While the chicken is browning, bring the water and 1 cup chicken broth to a boil in a medium-size saucepan. Add the rice; reduce the heat to medium-low, cover, and simmer until the rice is tender and all the liquid is absorbed, about 20 minutes.

4. In a small bowl, blend the remaining 1 cup broth with the reserved flour mixture. Add this and the soy sauce to the skillet and bring to a boil. Add the ginger, 3 tablespoons of the cilantro (if using), garlic, and honey. Reduce the heat to low, cover, and simmer for 10 minutes.

5. Return the chicken (and any juices on the plate) to the skillet. Spoon some of the sauce on the chicken, cover the pan, and simmer for another 5 minutes.

6. Meanwhile, in a small ungreased skillet, toast the sesame seeds over medium-low heat, shaking the pan frequently, about 3 minutes or until golden brown.

7. When the rice is done, stir in the toasted sesame seeds and remaining cilantro (if using). Serve the chicken with rice and sauce.

Serves 4

Ivana Trump

Fashion magnates and timeless beauties, Ivana and moi must have been separated at birth. Happily reunited, we now frequently share breakfast, lunch, and jewelry. We have so very much in common, except I wouldn't think of naming a recipe after a rain boot.

Ivana Trump's Beef Goulash

2 pounds beef shank or chuck,
   cut into 1-inch cubes

2 tablespoons all-purpose flour

1 to 3 teaspoons sweet
   Hungarian paprika

4 tablespoons (½ stick) unsalted
   butter or lard

2 tablespoons vegetable oil

2 medium-size yellow onions,
   minced

1 garlic clove, crushed

pinch of dried marjoram

salt

1 small green bell pepper, stemmed,
   seeded, and minced

1 medium-size tomato, peeled,
   seeded, and chopped

1 pound egg noodles

1. Preheat oven to 375°F.

2. Lightly dust the beef with the flour and paprika. Set a 3-
or 4-quart Dutch oven or flameproof casserole over high
heat and melt half of the butter with the oil. Add the beef
and sauté until browned, stirring constantly. Reduce the heat
to moderately high and add the onions and garlic. Cook until
the onions are translucent, 3 to 5 minutes. Add water to
cover (about 2 cups) and the marjoram and salt to taste.
Place the casserole in the oven and cook, uncovered, until the
beef is very tender, 1 to 1½ hours, stirring frequently. Add
more water if needed to prevent scorching.

3. Thirty minutes before the goulash is done, add the green
pepper and tomato.

4. Just before serving, cook the noodles in a large pot of
boiling salted water, according to package directions. Drain
and toss with the remaining 2 tablespoons butter.

5. Season the stew to taste with additional salt.
Serve at once with the hot, buttered noodles.

Serves 6

Yo-Yo Ma

Yo-Yo is a superb cellist. But not one word about his recipe for spareribs. Not one single word....

Yo-Yo Ma's Barbecued Spareribs with Beer and Honey

8 pounds pork spareribs, cut into serving-size pieces

3 cups beer

1 cup honey

2 teaspoons chili powder

1½ teaspoons dry mustard

2 teaspoons ground sage

1 teaspoon salt

2 tablespoons lemon juice

A Tip from Moi:
Skip the main course and go straight to dessert.

1. Place the ribs in a large shallow pan. Mix the remaining ingredients and pour over the ribs. Cover and let stand in the refrigerator for 24 hours, turning at least once.

2. Remove the ribs from the marinade, reserving the liquid. You can grill, broil, or bake the ribs. To grill, place them on the rack of a moderately hot charcoal grill 4 to 6 inches from the heat (for ease of turning, the ribs may be woven onto a spit or long skewers). Cook, turning frequently and brushing with the marinade, until brown, about 1¼ hours.

To broil the ribs, use the method above, positioning the broiler pan about 6 inches from the heat source.

To bake the ribs, preheat the oven to 325°F, place the ribs in a large baking pan, and bake, basting frequently, for about 1½ hours or until the ribs are brown and glazed.

With all three methods, take care that the glaze does not burn.

Serves 8

Jean Stapleton

*M*y dear, dear friend Jean is one of the sweetest, most endearing and talented stars in the entertainment industry. Although she has been a star for many years, she has never let fame go to her head. I wish I could be more like her....

Jean Stapleton's Sheba Casserole

1 medium-size onion, thinly sliced into rings

1 medium-size green bell pepper, stemmed, seeded, and thinly sliced into rings

1½ pounds sole fillets

1 cup sour cream

salt and pepper

1. Preheat oven to 350°F.

2. Cook onion rings and green pepper rings in boiling water until slightly soft. Drain. Wash the sole and pat dry. In a shallow casserole, layer the sole, vegetables, and sour cream, seasoning each layer with salt and pepper to taste and ending with sour cream.

3. Cover and bake for 25 to 30 minutes or until the fish is cooked and all is bubbly.

Serves 4

"I call this Sheba Casserole because it was introduced to me while on tour with the great Shirley Booth in Come Back, Little Sheba, *her Tony Award-winning role. A long road tour can bring a company together in a real family sense. Dinners are prepared and colleagues are invited. Wilson Brooks, a member of the company, made this casserole for the delight of his friends while we were playing in Chicago."*

–J. S.

A Tip from Moi:
What's fish without chips? Don't forget the fries!

James Galway's Thai-Cooked Prawns

1 pound tiger prawns

½ cup all-purpose flour
   or cornstarch

2 tablespoons vegetable oil

4 scallions, cut horizontally
   into slivers, white part
   separated from green tops

2 tablespoons red curry paste
   (recipe follows)

1 cup coconut milk (pour off
   and reserve the cream that
   will be separated on top)

2 to 3 tablespoons
   Thai fish sauce

2 tablespoons chopped
   palm sugar

6 kaffir lime leaves
   (dried or fresh)

fresh basil, finely shredded

cilantro, shredded

Red Curry Paste

2 tablespoons crushed red pepper
   flakes or 20 dried red Thai chilies

2 teaspoons white peppercorns

1 teaspoon cumin seeds

2 teaspoons coriander seeds

1 small red onion, chopped

3 garlic cloves, chopped

2 tablespoons fresh lemon grass,
   thinly sliced from lower end
   of stalk (discard roots)

2 tablespoons cilantro roots,
   well washed, chopped

1 teaspoon galangal powder or
   1 tablespoon fresh galangal,
   peeled and chopped

1 teaspoon grated lime zest

1 dried kaffir lime leaf

½ teaspoon shrimp paste

3 teaspoons sweet paprika

½ teaspoon turmeric

2 tablespoons vegetable oil

To prepare the curry paste:

1. If using the Thai chilies, wear rubber gloves to stem and seed them. Using scissors, snip into ½-inch pieces.

2. In a heavy skillet, dry-roast the peppercorns and seeds over moderate heat, stirring until fragrant. Let cool.

3. In a food processor, blend the peppercorns, seeds, and remaining ingredients except for the oil. Slowly add the oil in a steady stream until the paste has a smooth consistency.

James Galway and his wife, Jeanne

*D*earest James is a close friend and a world-class flautist. And as moi likes to say: If you got it, flaut it!

To prepare the prawns:

1. Peel and devein the prawns, discarding the heads and tails. Wash and pat dry. Lightly dust with the flour (this will seal in the flavor of the prawns). Set aside.

2. In a wok or large skillet, heat the oil over high heat until smoking. Add the white part of the scallions and the curry paste; cook, stirring, until fragrant. Add the reserved coconut cream and cook, stirring, until more fragrant. Add the prawns and coat well with the mixture. Add the coconut milk, cook until it comes to a boil, and then simmer for 1 minute. Add the fish sauce, palm sugar, and kaffir leaves; continue to simmer for 4 to 6 more minutes or until the prawns are cooked. (The cooking time will depend on the size of the prawns. Do not overcook. They should be firm to the touch.)

3. Before serving, remove and discard the kaffir leaves. Garnish with basil, cilantro, and the green part of the scallions.

Serves 2 to 4, depending on appetite

Note: Although homemade is always better, red curry paste can be purchased in Asian markets.

James Taylor

Darling Jimmy and I go way, way back. Many was the night he would serenade me on the beach…up on the roof…on a country road…in a traffic jam….

James Taylor's Baked Bluefish Fillets

2 teaspoons olive oil

1½ pounds bluefish fillets

2 tablespoons Dijon mustard

4 large garlic cloves, minced

½ teaspoon salt

freshly ground black pepper

1 medium-size onion, sliced into thin rings

3 tablespoons capers, drained

1 lemon, thinly sliced

1. Preheat oven to 375°F.

2. Brush 1 teaspoon olive oil over the bottom of a 9- by 13-inch baking dish. Lay fish fillets in the dish. Sprinkle the remaining olive oil over the fish. Brush the mustard over the fish and sprinkle with garlic, salt, and pepper to taste. Lay the onion rings on top and sprinkle with capers. Top with lemon slices. Cover with aluminum foil and bake 15 minutes, until the fish is firm and opaque.

Serves 4

A Tip from Moi:

Be the catch of the day! A blue dress and fishnet stockings go swimmingly with bluefish.

James Earl Jones

*My dear, dear Jimmy.
Moi has been wondering—
how do vous know that
the sea bass are from Chile?
Do they carry passports?*

James Earl Jones's Chilean Sea Bass

1 stick unsalted butter

10 Maui onions, sliced

12 Roma tomatoes, seeded and chopped
    (or the canned equivalent, drained)

5 shallots, chopped

3 garlic cloves, chopped

3 basil leaves, chopped

1 tablespoon extra-virgin olive oil

½ cup chicken broth (if necessary)

12 pieces (approximately 2 pounds) Chilean sea bass,
    each 2 inches wide by 2½ inches long

salt and white pepper

1. Preheat oven to 425°F.

2. Melt butter in a skillet on low heat. Add onions and cook until caramelized (1 to 2 hours). Meanwhile, purée tomatoes, shallots, garlic, and basil.

3. Heat oil in a pan. Add tomato purée and cook on low heat for 30 minutes or until sauce loses its watery texture. Add chicken broth if sauce becomes too thick.

4. Place sea bass in an ovenproof baking dish, season with salt and pepper, and top with caramelized onions. Bake for 10 to 12 minutes or until fish can be flaked with a fork.

5. Spoon sauce onto 6 plates. Place 2 pieces of onion-topped fish on sauce in each plate.

Serves 6

A Tip from Moi:

This recipe is great for those of you on a seafood diet. Moi always says, if you see food, eat it!

John Travolta

Dashing Johnny. No two people were ever more alike. We are both consummate actors. We both made the leap from TV to movie superstardom. And we both keep getting better-looking every year. Isn't destiny wonderful?

John Travolta's Lobster with Three Sauces

¼ cup white wine vinegar or apple cider vinegar

¼ cup olive oil or vegetable oil

1 heaping teaspoon fresh tarragon

½ teaspoon salt

3 garlic cloves, minced or crushed through a press

2 tablespoons plus 1 teaspoon Dijon mustard

¾ teaspoon pepper

3 tablespoons mayonnaise

2 tablespoons plain yogurt

2 tablespoons spicy brown mustard

¼ teaspoon dry mustard

¼ cup packed fresh basil or 2 teaspoons dried basil

2 scallions

1 tablespoon butter

½ cup sour cream

1 tablespoon fresh lemon juice

1½ tablespoons grated lemon zest (optional)

4 small lobsters (1 to 1¼ pounds each)

1. For the tarragon wine vinaigrette: In a small serving dish, combine the vinegar, oil, tarragon, salt, 1 of the garlic cloves, the 1 teaspoon Dijon mustard, and ¼ teaspoon pepper. If you prepare this sauce ahead of time, cover and refrigerate. Whisk before serving at room temperature.

2. For the creamy mustard sauce: In a small serving dish, combine the mayonnaise, yogurt, 2 tablespoons of the Dijon mustard, spicy brown mustard, dry mustard, and ¼ teaspoon of the pepper. If you make this sauce ahead of time, cover and refrigerate. Serve at room temperature.

3. For the lemon-herb sauce: Finely chop the basil and scallions. In a small skillet, melt the butter and add the remaining 2 garlic cloves. Cook until fragrant, about 1 minute. Add the basil and scallions and cook, stirring, until the scallions begin to soften, about 2 minutes. Take the skillet off the heat and stir in the sour cream, the remaining ¼ teaspoon pepper, lemon juice, and lemon zest (if using). Transfer the sauce to a small serving dish. Make this sauce just before serving and cover until ready to use.

4. If you don't want the bother of cooking the lobster yourself, the seafood counter is usually willing to do it for you. Otherwise, in a pot large enough to hold the lobsters, bring 5 inches of water to a boil. (If you don't have a large enough pot, cook the lobsters in batches.) Add the lobsters. Cover and return to a boil. Reduce heat to low and simmer until the lobsters are cooked through, about 10 minutes. Drain the lobsters well and serve with the three sauces.

Serves 4

Sensational Side Dishes and Sauces

◆

Supporting Rolls

Harry Belafonte knows how to handle hot stuff, and
he also has a great recipe for Corn Pudding on page 94.

Mary Steenburgen's Corn Spoon Bread

2 eggs, slightly beaten

1 8½-ounce package corn muffin mix

1 8-ounce can corn kernels, drained

1 8-ounce can creamed corn

1 cup dairy sour cream

½ cup butter or margarine, melted

½ cup shredded Swiss cheese

1. Preheat oven to 350°F.

2. Combine eggs, muffin mix, corn kernels, creamed corn, sour cream, and butter. Spread in an 11- by 7- by 1¾-inch baking dish. Bake for 35 minutes. Sprinkle cheese on top and bake for 10 to 15 more minutes or until a knife inserted in center comes out clean. Let cool for 15 minutes on a rack before cutting into squares.

Yield: 15 pieces, each about two inches square

A Tip from Moi:

Mary's spoon bread is a teensy bit fattening. Be sure to get someone to exercise for you, so you can eat this without worrying.

Mary Steenburgen

Mary is a wonderful actress and a dear, dear friend. I always enjoy seeing her in those lovely quiet-and-demure roles. Who would have thought her recipe for spoon bread would make moi want to party like a banshee?!

Melanie Griffith

*M*arvelous Melanie. We've been good friends ever since we auditioned for Working Girl. I was very close to getting the part until, at the last minute, they decided to cast some-one of the same species opposite Harrison Ford....

Melanie Griffith's Pesto Sauce for Pasta

3 cups lightly packed fresh basil

2 tablespoons coarsely chopped garlic (8 to 10 cloves)

1 cup extra-virgin olive oil

⅓ cup pine nuts

⅓ cup walnuts

¾ cup grated Parmesan cheese

salt and pepper to taste

3 tablespoons butter per pound of pasta, at room temperature (optional)

up to 3 pounds pasta of your choice

1. Just put all ingredients except the butter and pasta into a food processor or blender; purée to a fine paste. Stir in the butter (if using).

2. Cook the desired amount of pasta according to package directions. Reserve a little of the cooking water. Stir the water into the pesto and toss with the warm pasta. Serve right away.

Yield: 1½ cups, enough for 12 servings

The pesto can be divided into thirds and frozen for future use. Defrost a portion and bring it to room temperature before using.

A Tip from Moi:

Pesto makes a wonderful little topping for pasta, a sensational spread for sandwiches, and a dandy little car wax!

Betty Buckley

My lovely friend Betty is a magnificent singer and performer. But a culinary expert—who knew? Moi gives this recipe a rave review and an S.R.O.– whatever that means!

Betty Buckley's Parmesan Potatoes

12 small red potatoes (about 1½ pounds), unpeeled, sliced

4 garlic cloves, unpeeled

½ cup plus 2 tablespoons grated Parmesan cheese

4 tablespoons butter

2 tablespoons milk

½ teaspoon salt

¼ teaspoon pepper (preferably white)

2 tablespoons chopped parsley (optional)

1. Bring water to a boil in a 3-quart saucepan. Put in the potatoes and garlic and cook until the potatoes are tender, about 15 minutes.

2. Meanwhile, preheat the broiler. Butter a shallow 1-quart baking dish.

3. Drain the potatoes and garlic. When they're cool enough to handle, slip the garlic cloves out of their skins. In a shallow bowl, coarsely mash the potatoes and garlic with a potato masher or fork (do not use a food processor—it will make the potatoes gluey). Add ½ cup of the Parmesan, butter, milk, salt, and pepper. Spread the potato mixture in the baking dish and evenly sprinkle the remaining 2 tablespoons Parmesan over the top.

4. Broil 4 inches from the heat until the top is lightly browned, about 6 minutes. Serve the dish garnished with chopped parsley (if using).

Serves 6

Bryant Gumbel's Sweet Corn Succotash

10 strips bacon

6 garlic cloves, finely chopped

6 green onions, chopped

2 tablespoons butter

1 bell pepper, chopped

corn kernels cut from 15 ears
uncooked corn

1 15-ounce can lima beans

1 7-ounce jar roasted red peppers,
diced

1 large tomato, diced

salt and pepper

1. Fry the bacon until crispy. Remove the bacon from the pan and set aside. Pour off all but 1 tablespoon of the fat. In the same pan, sauté the garlic and onions until soft. Add the butter and bell pepper. Cook over medium heat until soft.

2. Add the corn and cook for 5 to 7 minutes or until tender. Add the lima beans, roasted red peppers, and tomato. Mix well. Crumble the bacon into the mix. Sprinkle with salt and pepper to taste.

Serves 10 to 12

Bryant Gumbel

Since Bryant is a dear, dear friend, moi will not comment about the unfortunate use of bacon in his recipe....

Frank Oz

*A*dorable Frank Oz has directed such big movies as **The Muppets Take Manhattan, Little Shop of Horrors, Dirty Rotten Scoundrels, What about Bob?, Housesitter,** *and* **Indian in the Cupboard.** *And although he hasn't cast me in any of his more recent block-busters, he still remains my biggest supporter....*

Frank Oz's Glop

1 pound frozen spinach

1 pound frozen chopped broccoli

4 zucchini, chopped

3 tablespoons margarine, cut into pieces

salt and pepper

1 8-ounce bag shredded mozzarella cheese

Spike vegetable seasoning
  (found in health food stores)

1. Preheat oven to 350°F.

2. In a large covered pot, steam spinach, broccoli, and zucchini in 1 cup water until done, 10 to 12 minutes. Drain.

3. In two batches, blend the vegetables in a food processor until mashed; add margarine and salt and pepper to taste. Put in a 6- to 8-cup casserole and sprinkle cheese on top.

4. Bake for 15 minutes or until cheese bubbles and browns. Sprinkle Spike on top and serve.

Serves 8

A Tip from Moi:

*If you are serving this dish to guests, you may want to give it a more elegant name such as **Glop Du Jour**, **Glop Jubilee**, or for extra special occasions, **Glop Suzette**.*

Maya Angelou

Moi has always admired my dear friend Maya Angelou. Just saying her name is fun! And her recipe is the best thing to happen to rice since weddings!

Maya Angelou's Jollof Rice
(a West African rice dish)

3 cups long-grain rice

6 tablespoons peanut oil

1 teaspoon salt

1 10½-ounce can beef consommé

about 3 cups water

1½ cups chopped onion

3 cups diced ham

1 28-ounce can whole tomatoes,
 diced, undrained

½ 6-ounce can tomato paste

2 dried hot red peppers, soaked in warm water

3 hard-cooked eggs, halved

¼ cup chopped parsley

To prepare:

1. Rinse rice in warm water, changing water until it is clear. Drain well.

2. In a 4-quart saucepan, heat 2 tablespoons of the oil and salt. Add ¾ cup of the rice. Cook, stirring frequently, until lightly browned, about 5 minutes. Add remaining rice, consommé, and enough water to cover rice by about an inch. Reduce heat to very, very low, cover, and simmer gently for 1 hour.

3. In a deep 10-inch skillet, heat remaining 4 tablespoons oil. Add onion and sauté until transparent. Stir in ham, tomatoes and their juice, and tomato paste. Cover and cook over medium heat 10 minutes. Drain off 1 cup of the liquid and reserve.

4. Remove peppers from their soaking liquid and squeeze them over rice. Add ham-tomato mixture, blending well. Cover and cook until liquid is absorbed, about 3 minutes. (If rice is too dry, add a bit of the reserved tomato liquid.)

To assemble:

Butter a 6- to 8-cup round mixing bowl. Arrange eggs, cut side down, in bottom of bowl. Sprinkle with parsley. Add rice mixture, packing firmly. Wait a few minutes to unmold. Turn out onto a serving plate.

Serves 8

Harry Belafonte

Handsome Harry and moi have worked together for many years. He has a lovely voice, a perfectly beautiful smile, and his recipe for corn pudding will leave you weak in the knees.

Harry Belafonte's Corn Pudding

(a southern delight)

4 large eggs

2 tablespoons cornstarch

4 tablespoons sugar

½ teaspoon salt

3 8½-ounce cans creamed corn

1½ cups milk

4 tablespoons butter, melted

2 tablespoons chopped onion
(optional)

1 teaspoon ground nutmeg

"This recipe seriously requires avoidance by those who are in pursuit of lowering their cholesterol. But even they must once in a while be tempted to indulge in some mouth-watering, lip-smacking mischief. See you at the weight factory."

—H. B.

1. Preheat oven to 300°F.

2. Separate the eggs. To the yolks add the cornstarch, sugar, and salt; blend thoroughly. Whisk in the corn, milk, and butter. Lightly sauté the onion (if using) and stir into the corn mixture. Beat the whites until stiff and fold in.

3. Pour into a 2-quart buttered casserole and set in a large dish or pan. Add enough hot water to the dish to come halfway up the sides of the casserole. Bake for 1 hour or until the top is golden brown and a knife inserted in the center comes out clean. Sprinkle with the nutmeg and let cool 20 minutes before serving.

Serves 8

Barbara Bush

Bar is such a dear, dear friend. I usually never have enough good things to say about her, but this recipe leaves me speechless....

Barbara Bush's Bologna for a Cocktail Buffet

1 5-pound roll beef bologna

½ cup French's mustard

2 tablespoons soy sauce

1 tablespoon dried rosemary

½ teaspoon ground ginger

2 tablespoons salad oil

hot biscuits

1. Preheat oven to 425°F.

2. Peel the bologna roll and make several 3-inch-long slashes across the top.

3. Mix the next five ingredients and spread over the bologna. Wrap in aluminum foil, place in a baking pan, and bake for 15 minutes. (An alternate method is to bake the bologna, uncovered, in a baking pan for about 20 minutes, occasionally basting with the sauce.) Transfer to a hot platter. Slice and serve on biscuits. Delicious!!!

Serves a lot

Charles is as warm and comforting as these yummy biscuits. Over the years, Charles often asked moi to accompany him on the road, but his Winnebago just wasn't big enough for all my cosmetics cases.

Charles Kuralt

"These are the best I ever tasted!"
–C. K.

Charles Kuralt's Sour Cream Biscuits

2 cups all-purpose flour, sifted

4 teaspoons baking powder

½ teaspoon salt

½ teaspoon cream of tartar

½ cup (1 stick) butter

1 cup sour cream

2 teaspoons milk

1. Preheat oven to 450°F.

2. Mix the dry ingredients with butter until the whole mixture has the consistency of BBs *(or very small peas, if you don't know what BBs are).*

3. With a fork, stir in the sour cream and milk until evenly mixed.

4. Knead gently.

5. Roll out the dough on a floured board to a thickness of ¾ inch to 1 inch.

6. Cut dough into biscuits with a biscuit cutter or a small glass.

7. Bake biscuits on an ungreased baking sheet for 12 minutes or until golden. Serve hot, if you can.

Makes 12 three-inch biscuits

The unbaked biscuits freeze well and will keep for a week to 10 days in the freezer. Bake at 450°F for 20 minutes if you bake them from the freezer.

"Ed Koren"

*E*ddie is such a wonderful cartooniste. And
The New Yorker is one of the few good pieces of
literature left in New York. But, if you really want to
know, it could use horoscopes, personals, and a few
of those lovely free perfume samples....

Ed Koren's Pond Village Pesto

2 cups packed fresh basil

½ cup good olive oil

2 tablespoons pine nuts

2 or 3 garlic cloves

1 teaspoon salt or to taste

1 cup freshly grated Parmesan cheese

"Just the right amount for about one pound of pasta— also spread on toast, toss with potatoes, whatever you like."
—E. K.

1. Put basil, oil, pine nuts, garlic, and salt in a food processor or blender. Mix at high speed. Scrape ingredients down toward the bottom with a rubber spatula and blend again.

2. Put the blended ingredients into a bowl and stir in the cheese by hand.

3. If you are using this pesto as a sauce for pasta, add a tablespoon or two of boiling water from the pasta pot and mix—this makes the sauce cling to the pasta more evenly.

Yield: 1 cup

Note: The pesto freezes extremely well. However, it tastes a lot better if you freeze it after Step 1 (before you put in the cheese). Stir in the cheese after it has defrosted.

Beverly Sills's Foolproof Hollandaise Sauce

3 eggs

¼ pound (1 stick) butter

3 tablespoons lemon juice

salt to taste

1. Heat water in the bottom of a double boiler until lightly boiling.

2. Mix all the ingredients at high speed in a blender. Pour mixture into the top of the double boiler and heat, whisking vigorously and constantly until thickened.

Yield: 1¼ cups

A Tip from Moi:

Hollandaise is delicious on all kinds of foods: broccoli, fish, and eggs. But don't be a fuddy-duddy with your hollandaise; be bold, dunk your pretzels in it!

Beverly Sills

*S*weet Beverly and I first met at the Carnegie–the deli,
not the hall. She is a wonderful lady, a dear, close personal
friend, and a true professional. She taught me everything
I know about music–unfortunately she didn't teach me
everything she knows....

Divine Desserts

◆

Heaven

Martha Stewart and Miss Piggy cook up a recipe
for Gingerbread on page 116. *Now that's living!*

Ben and Jerry

Dearest Ben and Jerry are the nicest combination to come along since cookies and cream. Your ice creams are sinfully delicious! By the way, boys, as long as you're reading this, I don't care what the label says, there are not four servings in those teensy pints.

Ben and Jerry's Superfudge Brownies

4 ounces unsweetened chocolate

½ cup (1 stick) butter

4 large eggs, at room temperature

½ teaspoon salt

2 cups sugar

1 teaspoon vanilla extract

1 cup all-purpose flour

1. Preheat oven to 350°F. Butter and lightly flour a 9- by 13-inch baking pan.

2. Melt the chocolate and butter in the top of a double boiler over simmering water. Let cool in the pan to room temperature. (If you're in a hurry, you can quickly cool it in the refrigerator, but be sure it doesn't become solid again.)

3. Beat the eggs and salt in a mixing bowl until very fluffy. Gradually beat in the sugar and vanilla. Gently fold in the cooled chocolate mixture. Add the flour and fold in just until blended. (It is important to fold in the chocolate and flour gently to keep the batter as fluffy as possible.)

4. Pour the batter into the prepared baking pan and smooth the top. Bake 25 to 30 minutes. Let cool completely in the pan before cutting.

Yield: 9 brownies, each about 3 by 4 inches

A Tip from Moi:

This simple dessert is perfect. I wouldn't add anything to it...except maybe a teensy scoop of ice cream. And what's ice cream without hot fudge sauce? And you can't have hot fudge sauce without whipped cream. And if you're going to add whipped cream, you may as well put a cherry on top!

Plácido Domingo

Incredible tenor Plácido—what fun we've had working together. Darling Plácido has always told moi that my voice was unlike anything he'd ever heard before…flatterer!

Plácido Domingo's Crème Chocolat

½ pound sweet chocolate (finely chopped or chocolate bits)

1½ cups heavy cream

1 tablespoon plus ½ teaspoon sugar

2 eggs

1½ teaspoons vanilla

1. Melt the chocolate in a double boiler. Add 1 cup of the cream and 1 tablespoon of the sugar, slowly stirring until the mixture is smooth and the sugar is dissolved. Remove from the heat. Separate the eggs. In a large bowl, lightly beat the yolks with the ½ teaspoon sugar. Slowly add the egg yolk mixture to the chocolate mixture. Add 1 teaspoon of the vanilla and stir again.

2. Beat the egg whites and the remaining ½ teaspoon vanilla until the whites form peaks. Fold into the chocolate mixture. Cover and refrigerate.

3. Whip the remaining ½ cup cream. Serve the dessert chilled, topped with whipped cream. This is a very rich dessert and should be presented in modest quantities.

Serves 4

If you are concerned about the possible health risks of raw eggs, substitute an additional ½ cup heavy cream (whipped to soft peaks) for the egg whites. The yolks are sufficiently cooked.

Shopping list
chocolate
heavy cream
sugar
eggs
vanilla

Gael Greene

*M*oi is proud to share this recipe from Gael Greene, trusted food critic and founder of Citymeals-on-Wheels. Unlike darling Gael, moi could never be critical of food. In fact I never met a meal I didn't like!

Gael Greene's Famous Fruit Crumble

nonstick cooking spray

3 pint-size boxes blueberries, picked over for stems and soft berries; or 4 cups sliced plums, nectarines, or Granny Smith apples

½ cup granulated sugar (more if the plums are sort of sour)

3 tablespoons fresh orange juice

1 tablespoon instant tapioca

½ cup firmly packed brown sugar

¾ cup all-purpose flour

1 tablespoon canola oil

½ cup rolled oats or Grape Nuts

1. Preheat oven to 350°F.

2. Spray an 8- by 8-inch glass baking dish with nonstick cooking spray. Put fruit in a bowl. Add granulated sugar, 1 tablespoon of the orange juice, and tapioca. Mix well with a wooden spoon. Dump fruit mixture into the baking dish.

3. Mix brown sugar and flour by hand or in a food processor. Add oil and remaining 2 tablespoons orange juice. Mix again or pulse in the food processor until it bunches up a bit. Remove blade. Stir in oats or Grape Nuts. Spoon topping over fruit, covering it as much as you can. Bake 20 to 30 minutes until fruit is soft and top is a little golden. Some people like to plop mock crème fraîche (see recipe) or whipped cream on top.

Serves 8 to 12

Mock Crème Fraîche

This is like whipped cream but smoother, like a soft snowdrift. And it has no fat at all.

¼ cup firmly packed brown sugar

1 teaspoon vanilla

⅔ cup plain nonfat yogurt

Stir brown sugar and vanilla into yogurt in a pretty pitcher or small bowl. Wrap in plastic wrap and let it sit in the fridge at least 20 minutes to melt any sugar bumps. Stir again before serving. I like this on any kind of fruit, cooked or raw, and on pound cake, too.

Lena Horne's Strawberry and Champagne Sorbet

2 cups (about ¾ pound)
   hulled strawberries, quartered
   and chilled

¾ cup sugar

2 tablespoons fresh lemon juice

2 cups chilled dry Champagne

6 ripe strawberries for garnish

1. Put the strawberry quarters, sugar, and lemon juice in a food processor or blender; process the mixture briefly so that the berries are finely chopped but not puréed. Add the Champagne, pouring it slowly against the inside of the bowl to keep it from frothing. Blend quickly to retain as much effervescence as possible.

2. Pour the mixture into a shallow nonreactive metal pan and put it in the freezer. Every 20 minutes take it out and stir or break it up with a fork until there is no juice left, just sludge (1½ to 2 hours). Scoop into dessert glasses. Garnish with reserved strawberries, and serve with a glass of chilled Champagne.

Serves 6

Lena Horne

*O*nly someone as refined as my dear, dear friend
Lena could come up with a recipe as elegant as this
little sorbet. But Lena, dearest, how could you forget
the chocolate sprinkles?!

Tom Brokaw's Granola

Tom Brokaw

*T*ommy is the ideal man, if you ask moi. He's intelligent, good-looking, and you can always count on him being in the same place at the same time, every night!

2 cups pitted dates, prunes, raisins, or other dried fruit (apricots, cherries, pineapple, cranberries, currants)

4 cups old-fashioned rolled oats

1 cup shredded coconut

1 cup pine nuts or coarsely chopped walnuts

1 cup wheat germ

⅓ cup sesame seeds

½ cup honey

½ cup oil

½ teaspoon salt (optional)

1. Preheat oven to 325°F.

2. With scissors, snip fruit into small pieces and set aside.

3. Combine oats, coconut, nuts, wheat germ, and sesame seeds in a large bowl. Stir honey and oil in a saucepan; heat to a boil. Stir honey-oil combination into oats mixture; mix well. Spread in two 10- by 15-inch baking pans. Bake for 25 minutes, stirring occasionally. Remove from oven and mix in fruit. Sprinkle with salt (if using).

Yield: approximately 1½ pounds

I love dear Tony's recipe because there is no cooking involved and because Camembert is French—I think. But what the heck is a Comice pear?

Tony Randall

Tony Randall's Favorite Pear Dessert

"My favorite dessert is a pear—a ripe, ripe Comice, served with cheese. A soft Brie or Camembert is delicious, but so is a sharp Cheddar and much healthier."

– T. R.

To prepare: Choose 2 very ripe Comice pears and 2 to 3 ounces of your favorite cheese. Let the cheese sit on the kitchen counter until it reaches room temperature. When the cheese is ready, peel, core, and quarter the pears. Cut the cheese into wedges. Arrange each pear on a plate with a wedge of cheese. Serve this immediately. If it is allowed to sit too long, the pears will turn brown.

Serves 2

Kermit the Frog

*K*ermie, Kermie, Kermie—
my sweet little Kermie. There's
no way I would ever eat anything called grasshopper pie!

Kermit's Favorite Grasshopper Pie

Crust

1½ cups crushed Oreos (about 16 cookies)

2 tablespoons melted butter

Filling

⅓ cup milk

1 package unflavored gelatin

½ cup sweetened condensed milk

⅓ cup crème de menthe

⅓ cup crème de cacao

1¼ cups heavy cream

Topping

½ cup heavy cream

chocolate curls or shavings
    (pick the chocolate of your choice—
    semisweet, bittersweet, or milk)

To make the crust:

In a small bowl, stir together the Oreos and butter. Press onto the bottom and sides of a 9-inch pie dish. Refrigerate until ready to use.

To make the filling:

1. Put the milk into a small heatproof bowl and sprinkle the gelatin over it. Set aside for 5 minutes. In a medium-size bowl, whisk together the condensed milk, crème de menthe, and crème de cacao. Set aside.

2. Set the bowl of milk and gelatin over a small pan of boiling water or use a double boiler and stir gently until smooth, about 4 minutes. Whisk into the condensed milk mixture. Refrigerate the filling, stirring often, until it begins to set, 30 to 40 minutes. Whip the 1¼ cups cream until stiff and fold it into the filling. Spoon into the pie crust and refrigerate for at least 2 hours.

To serve:

Whip the ½ cup cream and decorate the top of the pie. Sprinkle with chocolate curls.

"I prefer mine sprinkled with a dozen caramelized crickets."

—K. F.

Yield: 1 nine-inch pie

Martha Stewart's Gingerbread

½ pound (2 sticks) margarine

1 cup dark brown sugar

1¼ cups unsulfured molasses

3 eggs

8 to 9 cups sifted all-purpose
  flour

1 tablespoon baking soda

1 teaspoon salt

1 teaspoon ground allspice

1 teaspoon ground cinnamon

1 teaspoon ground cloves

1 teaspoon ground ginger

1. Cream margarine and sugar until smooth. Add molasses and eggs. Beat until smooth.

2. Sift 3 cups of the flour with the baking soda, salt, and spices. Gradually beat into the sugar mixture. Add 5 to 6 cups more flour, beating until just mixed. Dough will be heavy and stiff. Form into 2 flat disks, wrap in plastic wrap, and chill at least 2 hours.

3. Preheat oven to 350°F.

For cookies:

1. On a lightly floured board, roll dough ⅛ inch thick. Cut out cookies and place on parchment-covered baking sheets.

2. Bake for 10 to 15 minutes, until done but not browned.

For houses:

1. Butter baking sheets (the sheets should be flat, with no edges, and large enough to hold the largest shape).

2. Roll dough right on tray and cut out shapes, leaving at least 1½ inches between shapes. Remove excess dough.

3. Bake until done, 10 minutes or longer depending on size of pieces.

Yield: about 10 dozen cookies of various sizes and shapes

© *ENTERTAINING by Martha Stewart, 1982*
Published by Clarkson N. Potter, Inc.
201 East 50th Street
New York, NY 10022

Martha Stewart

*M*agnificent Martha is the absolute do-it-yourselfer. She grows her own herbs, she knits her own doilies, she builds her own gingerbread houses. On my birthday she even sent moi a full-scale chocolate sculpture of moi's own self. It was almost too beautiful to eat. Almost....

"Perfect for cutout cookies and gingerbread houses."
—M. S.

Gene Shalit

"Skip the picture; eat the cake."
–G. S.

*T*he critics won't pan this crumb cake. The beginning was exciting and had moi glued to the kitchen counter. The middle was filling and very satisfying. And in the end, the topping topped it off. This cake will rise to any occasion!

Gene Shalit's Movie Crumb Cake

1. Before going to the theater, preheat oven to 325°F. (Note: postheat not recommended.) While waiting, grease a 9-inch-square cake pan.

Filling and Topping:

2. In a medium bowl, mix

> $\frac{1}{3}$ cup packed brown sugar
>
> $\frac{1}{4}$ cup granulated white sugar
>
> 1 teaspoon cinnamon
>
> 3 tablespoons margarine (this must be exact; do not leave any margarine for error)

Cut in margarine with a pastry blender until it's crumbly.

2½. Set aside. (After all that, you *set it aside*. What a recipe.)

3. In a large (not big, not huge, a *large*) bowl, mix until very smooth

> ½ cup soft margarine
>
> 1 cup sugar
>
> 2 eggs (out of shells)
>
> 1 teaspoon baking soda
>
> 1 teaspoon baking powder
>
> ¼ teaspoon salt
>
> 1 teaspoon vanilla extract

4. Then—and only then—slowly, verrrrry slowly—mix in

> 2 cups sifted flour
>
> 1 cup sour cream (why do they put a date on sour cream?)

Alternate the flour and sour cream additions, starting and ending with flour. Just blend; don't overmix.

5. Spread half of this mixture in prepared pan. (I have no idea what a prepared pan is. Most pans are unprepared and are often caught off guard.)

6. Sprinkle half of topping (you remember the topping—that stuff up in the first paragraph marked 2).

7. Place remaining batter (this is the first I hear of "batter." Where did this come from?) on top of crumb mixture (2—very busy number).

8. Top (that's a verb, i.e., to Top) with remaining crumb mixture (how much of this stuff *is* there?).

9. Place everything—square pans, prepared pans, unprepared pans, topping, bottoming, crumbs—the whole business, in oven (which by this time better be at 325°F or else you're going to need a new oven) and set timer (I forgot to tell you, you need a timer) for 40 minutes.

10. Test for doneness. (Check dictionary for "doneness.")

Donate cake to neighbor and go to the movies.

Gen. Norman Schwarzkopf

$\mathcal{M}$oi's favorite mission with Stormy Normie was the night we raided his refrigerator. He is my favorite general—not counting General Foods and General Mills.

General Schwarzkopf's Sour Cream Peach Pie

1 16-ounce can sliced peaches, packed in water, thoroughly drained

1 9-inch deep-dish pie shell, unbaked

1/3 cup all-purpose flour

1/2 cup plus 1 tablespoon sugar

1/4 teaspoon salt

1 cup sour cream

1/2 teaspoon ground cinnamon

1. Preheat oven to 350°F.

2. Arrange peaches in pie shell, reserving one slice for garnish, if desired. In a medium-size bowl, whisk together flour, 1/2 cup of the sugar, salt, and sour cream. Spoon mixture over peaches. Combine cinnamon and remaining sugar and sprinkle over top. Bake 30 to 40 minutes, until crust is lightly browned. If using, garnish with reserved peach slice cut into thin wedges.

Serves 10

A Tip from Moi:

To make this a Dessert Storm, bombard it with several scoops of vanilla ice cream.

Willard Scott

*D*ear, sweet Willard is one of my very closest friends. In fact Kermit and Willard started out together in the early days of live TV—of course, moi is much too young to remember those days. I mean, get real! They didn't even have informercials back then....

Willard Scott's Brown Sugar Pound Cake

5 eggs

½ pound (2 sticks) butter

½ cup Crisco shortening

1 pound plus 1 cup firmly packed light brown sugar

3½ cups all-purpose flour

½ teaspoon baking powder

1 cup milk

1. Preheat oven to 325°F.

2. Let eggs and butter sit until they're at room temperature. Cream together butter and shortening. Add eggs, one at a time, beating after each addition until smooth. Add brown sugar and blend thoroughly.

3. Sift together flour and baking powder. Alternating ingredients, add flour mixture and milk to batter, beginning and ending with dry ingredients. Bake in a greased and floured 10-inch tube pan for 1¼ to 1½ hours. Let cool on a rack for 1 hour before removing from pan.

Frosting

1 cup finely chopped pecans

¼ pound (1 stick) butter

1 box powdered sugar

milk to thin

While cake is cooling, turn oven to broil. Toast pecans in butter in a thick broiler pan or an 8- by 8-inch baking pan, stirring occasionally, until nuts are well browned. Watch them closely; don't allow them to burn. Let cool a little; then add powdered sugar. Add enough milk to thin frosting to spreading consistency. Spread on top of cake. Some should drip down sides and center, but it should not be spread anywhere except on top.

Sally/Test kitchen
see what you
can do with
this one —
Miss Piggy
XXX

Calvin Trillin's Scrambled Eggs That Stick to the Pan Every Time

This is my only dish. I used to turn it out every school morning for my two daughters. They hated it. When they got old enough, they announced to me that they would never eat my scrambled eggs again.

Ingredients:
    Eggs
    Milk, if you can find it (back behind the lettuce, hidden by the shadow of the Chinese take-out leftovers)
    Butter

1. Burn the butter while looking for sandwich bread for lunch or discussing riboflavin content of various cereals.
2. Apologize to daughters for your language.
3. Put a little milk (if you can find it) with the eggs, and shove the eggs around in the pan until you remember that the toast is about to burn.
4. Turn back to the eggs, which by this time have stuck to the pan.
5. Serve with burnt toast and a wan smile.

PICTURE CREDITS

The sources for the illustrations that appear in this book are listed below.
Credits from left to right are separated by semicolons, from top to bottom by dashes.

Cover: front, John E. Barrett; back, John E. Barrett—Steven Mays; Courtesy John Travolta; Renée Comet (©1996 Time-Life Books); ©1993 CNN, Inc. All Rights Reserved, Andrew Eccles/Outline/Courtesy Larry King; Courtesy Candice Bergen; Ellen Silverman. **3:** Renée Comet (©1996 Time-Life Books). **4:** Renée Comet (©1986 Time-Life Books)—Renée Comet (©1996 Time-Life Books). **5:** Renée Comet (©1996 Time-Life Books)—John E. Barrett. **7-8:** John E. Barrett. **9:** From *The Object Series,* PhotoDisc, Inc., USA, Seattle, Washington. **10:** John E. Barrett—Renée Comet (©1996 Time-Life Books). **11:** Renée Comet (©1996 Time-Life Books). **13:** Ellen Wallop—From *The Object Series,* PhotoDisc, Inc., USA, Seattle, Washington (2). **14:** Ellen Wallop—John E. Barrett. **15:** John E. Barrett. **16:** Steve Crise. **17:** Renée Comet (©1996 Time-Life Books). **18:** Renée Comet (©1996 Time-Life Books). **19:** © Archive Photos. **20:** Courtesy Katie Couric; Alan Richardson. **22:** John E. Barrett. **23:** Courtesy Cheryl Tiegs; Renée Comet (©1996 Time-Life Books). **24:** Courtesy Brooke Shields; Renée Comet (©1996 Time-Life Books). **25:** John E. Barrett. **26:** Renée Comet (©1996 Time-Life Books). **27:** ©1993 CNN, Inc. All Rights Reserved, Andrew Eccles/Outline/ Courtesy Larry King; Renée Comet (©1996 Time-Life Books). **28:** Bob Thomas/© Archive Photos. **29:** Walter Weissman/Globe Photos, Inc. **31:** Renée Comet (©1986 Time-Life Books). **32:** Courtesy Matt Lauer; Renée Comet (©1986 Time-Life Books). **34:** John E. Barrett. **35:** Renée Comet (©1996 Time-Life Books). **37:** Courtesy Candice Bergen; Ellen Silverman. **38:** Popperfoto/© Archive Photos. **40:** © Adam Scull/Globe Photos, Inc.; Renée Comet (©1996 Time-Life Books). **42:** Courtesy Robin Leach. **43:** From *The Object Series,* PhotoDisc, Inc., USA, Seattle, Washington. **44:** Renée Comet (©1996 Time-Life Books)/PLAYBILL®is a registered trademark of Playbill Incorporated, NYC. Used by permission. **45:** Courtesy Diane Sawyer; Renée Comet (©1996 Time-Life Books). **46:** Courtesy Samuel L. Jackson; Renée Comet (©1996 Time-Life Books). **48:** Renée Comet (©1996 Time-Life Books). **49:** Brian J. Gill/Globe Photos, Inc. **50:** Lisa Rose/Globe Photos, Inc. ©1994. **51:** Adam Scull/Globe Photos, Inc. ©1990. **52:** Courtesy Glenn Close; Steven Mark Needham. **54:** Andrea Renault/Globe Photos, Inc. **55:** Renée Comet (©1996 Time-Life Books). **56:** John E. Barrett. **57:** Renée Comet (©1996 Time-Life Books); Ralph Dominguez/Globe Photos, Inc. **58:** Ellen Wallop. **59:** Courtesy Pierre Franey. **60:** Henry

McGee/Globe Photos, Inc.; Renée Comet (©1996 Time-Life Books). **62:** Ralph Dominguez/Globe Photos, Inc. **63:** Steven Mark Needham. **64:** Adam Scull/Globe Photos, Inc. ©1992. **65:** Alan Richardson. **66:** Archive Photos; Renée Comet (©1996 Time-Life Books). **68:** J. Henry Fair/Courtesy Yo-Yo Ma; John E. Barrett. **69:** Renée Comet (©1996 Time-Life Books). **70:** Lisa Rose/Globe Photos, Inc. ©1995. **71:** John E. Barrett. **73:** Courtesy James and Jeanne Galway. **74:** © Adam Scull/Globe Photos, Inc. ©1981; Renée Comet (©1996 Time-Life Books). **75:** John E. Barrett. **76:** Michael Jacobs/Courtesy James Earl Jones. **77:** John E. Barrett. **78:** Courtesy John Travolta. **79:** Steven Mays. **80:** Ellen Wallop. **81:** Renée Comet (©1996 Time-Life Books). **82:** John E. Barrett. **83:** Courtesy Mary Steenburgen; Renée Comet (©1996 Time-Life Books). **84:** Greg Gorman/ Courtesy Melanie Griffith. **85:** John E. Barrett. **86:** Archive Photos; Steven Mark Needham. **89:** Courtesy Bryant Gumbel; Renée Comet (©1996 Time-Life Books)—Ellen Wallop. **90:** Courtesy Frank Oz. **91:** John E. Barrett. **92:** Courtesy Maya Angelou. **93:** Renée Comet (©1996 Time-Life Books). **94:** Courtesy Harry Belafonte; Renée Comet (©1996 Time-Life Books). **96:** Official White House Photograph/Courtesy Barbara Bush. **97:** Walter Weissman/Globe Photos, Inc. ©1994. **98:** Courtesy Ed Koren; Renée Comet (©1996 Time-Life Books). **100:** John E. Barrett. **101:** Renée Comet (©1996 Time-Life Books); Bachrach/Courtesy Beverly Sills. **102:** C. Todd Eberle. **103:** Renée Comet (©1996 Time-Life Books). **104:** Courtesy Ben Cohen and Jerry Greenfield. **105:** John E. Barrett. **106:** Peter Weissbech/Courtesy Plácido Domingo; Renée Comet (©1996 Time-Life Books). **107:** Renée Comet (©1996 Time-Life Books). **108:** Courtesy Gael Greene. **111:** Renée Comet (© 1986 Time-Life Books); Cleo Sullivan/Courtesy Lena Horne. **112:** Courtesy Tom Brokaw. **113:** Courtesy Tony Randall; Renée Comet (©1996 Time-Life Books). **114:** John E. Barrett. **115:** Renée Comet (©1996 Time-Life Books). **117:** Renée Comet (©1996 Time-Life Books); Kurt Stier/Courtesy Martha Stewart. **118:** Courtesy Gene Shalit. **119:** From *The Object Series,* PhotoDisc, Inc., USA, Seattle, Washington. **120:** Courtesy General Norman Schwarzkopf; Renée Comet (©1996 Time-Life Books). **121:** John E. Barrett. **122:** Dariene Hammond/© Archive Photos. **123:** Renée Comet (©1996 Time-Life Books). **124:** Renée Comet (©1996 Time-Life Books)—Rose Hartman/Globe Photos, Inc. ©1994.

INDEX

INDEX

ACKNOWLEDGMENTS

Miss Piggy had a teensy bit of help from Alison Inches and Craig Shemin at Jim Henson Productions, Inc.

Miss Piggy would also like to thank Duke Zeibert for lending Larry King his Tuna Health Salad recipe and recipe-contest winner Beverley Ann Crummey for creating Paul Newman's Tasty Thai Shrimp and Sesame Noodles dish. Other folks who lent a hand are Esther del Rosario, Brian Dittmar, Phil George, Mimi Harrison, and Cathy Tyson.

Time-Life Custom Publishing

Vice President and Publisher
Terry Newell

Project Editor
Sally Collins

Food Consultant
Lisa Cherkasky

Director of New Product Development
Regina Hall

Director of Sales
Neil Levin

Managing Editor
Donia Steele

Production Manager
Carolyn Bounds

Quality Assurance Manager
James D. King

Design by Miles Fridberg Molinaroli, Inc.

Books produced by Time-Life Custom Publishing are available at special bulk discount for corporate and promotional use. Call 1-800-323-5255.